ANCHOR
BOOKS

BATTLE LINES

Edited by

Rachael Radford

First published in Great Britain in 2003 by
ANCHOR BOOKS
Remus House,
Coltsfoot Drive,
Peterborough, PE2 9JX
Telephone (01733) 898102

HB ISBN 1 84418 072 7
SB ISBN 1 84418 073 5

FOREWORD

Anchor Books is a small press, established in 1992, with the aim of promoting readable poetry to as wide an audience as possible.

We hope to establish an outlet for writers of poetry who may have struggled to see their work in print.

The poems presented here have been selected from many entries, and as always editing proved to be a difficult task.

I trust this selection will delight and please the authors and all those who enjoy reading poetry.

Rachael Radford
Editor

CONTENTS

A SAD DAY, USA
(11th September 2001)

We've lived in peace for some years now
No more wars were the wise men's view,
But lo and behold they're back again
The people who seem to have no shame
Hijacking a plane flying into skyscrapers tall
Innocent people on board they killed them all.
We watched in horror the event on TV
A terrible sight for us all to see
Who did this awful thing people say
We mustn't let them get away
It's not the same as hunting the *Hun,*
They live in caves causing lots of strife
And don't give a darn for human life
We mustn't cause them too much mayhem
We don't want to be classed like them
So we'll wait, be quiet and pliant
Do they realise they have woken a sleeping giant?
Peace in our time Winston Churchill said
We must keep that saying in our head
But the Americans started a bombing campaign
I really think they must be insane,
The terrorists have all run away
Leaving innocent people caught in the fray
How long will it last we begin to wonder
Let's hope we don't see the world broke asunder
We must all hope that when we pray
The Lord will see us through each day.

Pat Cook

THE SOLDIER'S PLEA

Sleep so gently, oh, my lovely
    I'll be gone before you wake
For the time has come for parting
    And my heart with love does ache.
Yesterday, before the altar
    We stood proudly side by side
And we vowed our love eternal
    That's when you became my bride.

Dream so sweetly oh my darling
    For the night will quickly pass
Keep the mem'ry oh so tightly
    When we meet at Candlemas.
Then by Eastertide we said we
    Would be married by next spring -
Never dreaming I'd be called to war,
    When I gave you my ring.

Oh breath softly oh, my sweetheart
    I can hear the catch of tears -
For last night you sobbed until you slept,
    You told me all your fears.
But the world still loves a lover
    And I know God feels the same
And he'll keep me safe from danger
    Till I'm home your heart to claim.

Sleep so easily my dearest -
    Slumber deep until the morn.
Though the night-time's ragged curtain
    Is pulled back by early dawn.
I must go to face the cannon
    Rifle fire and musket shell -
But I promise you, my darling
    I'll come home to you from hell.

One last kiss upon your forehead
    From our bed I now must creep.
I'll tread softly on the staircase
    For I'll not disturb your sleep.
To the meeting point I must go
    Though with heavy steps I'll take -
So sleep sweetly, oh, my lovely
    I'll be gone before you wake.

Pamela R Dalton

WAR AND PEACE

God gave free-will to man to choose
Which was his way:
And arrogance and pride to lose,
And say them, 'Nay'.

But man desir'd the victor's crown,
By sword and fire;
He cared not if his foes were down -
He did not tire.

But some there are with peace at heart,
Cost what it may,
And, ruled by love, hate has no part
It now can play!

Ruth Shallard

SEPTEMBER 11TH 2001

That fateful day affected us all,
Even if we had no loved ones involved, none at all.
What on earth did it all achieve?
Can anyone tell me, please?
How many innocent lives were taken,
And all because of one man, Bin Laden.

That day will stay with us forever,
People will not forget, never
Because of all those people lost,
And tell me now, at what cost?
Such a devastating shock it was,
Everyone feels each other's loss.

The whole world came together,
To unite in need, whatever, whenever:
Differences put aside at last,
This date now in history, now is past.
Come together and help one another,
For we are as one, sister and brother.

Louise Lee

I DOUBT IT

Three quarters of the world's at war,
At any given time,
But the war I've got to deal with,
Is the war that's only mine.

I can't say no to anyone,
And I'm run right off my feet.
I think I'm fat, I try to slim,
And then find more to eat.

I know I need some exercise
But, no, it's not for me.
I cannot run, I cannot walk,
I've a car to drive you see.

I know I really shouldn't smoke,
But haven't the will to stop.
And if I carry on like this,
It'll be my clogs I'll pop.

I wonder if the government,
Would like to intervene,
And see if they can stop my war,
While I'm still on the scene.

Elaine Morris

A PEACEFUL HEART

Where will you find the peace you crave for?
Down by the river where the otters play.
Or maybe the waves crashing over the sand
with the sun going down at the end of the day.

Maybe you'll find it among the dark trees,
their leafy arms reaching up on high.
Or it could be the sound of a favourite tune,
or a lark ascending into the sky.

Away from the noise of the traffic and smoke,
one can feel worries and cares slip away.
Just to relax and unwind is the thing.
A change from the worries and cares of today.

A warm summer night and a soft gentle breeze.
Surely a gift and a balm to the mind.
Swans on the river, grass under our feet,
this is the time to enjoy and unwind.

All of these blessings are food for the soul
but when the day's over we have to depart.
Joy though it has been, we must carry on,
for surely the real peace must be in your heart.

Joan Cooke

THE UNIVERSE

The wonder of the universe
how did it all begin?
Some say 'twas evolution
some say 'twas the mortal sin.

In darkness was the world of ours
God said, 'Let there be light!'
The darkness night, the light is day
children of God will sing hooray!

Water next and earth so strong
the seeds of fruit were planted
man knows that he can sing his song
in praise for what God has granted.

The sun and moon were next created
the stars filled the great sky
oh Lord you are so highly rated
so why then must man cry?

Man is cruel to all this power
hatred spreading wide
reducing Earth each hour by hour
no longer can there be pride.

Pollution in the sky and seas
your universe cut down
destroying Earth why should it be
where is the glory crown?

Death of humans near and far
starvation and disease
the world seems like one big war
for whom we all must grieve.

Why Lord must we then destroy
what you took care to make
what really should bring so much joy
the world you did create.

Whichever way we look at it
the wanting and the greed
each one of us should sit and think
for Lord we are in need.

In need of your forgiveness
for making things go wrong
for Lord you know of all this mess
where will we all belong?

The wonder of the universe
and will it ever end
the world under one big curse
Lord will it ever mend?

Susan Sissons

1642

They've cut the grass since last I came,
Active once, but now I'm lame.

This house was mine, the grounds were vast,
I thought my tenancy would last,
I thought my years of living here,
Would grow and spread, I felt no fear.
Young I was, and filled with strength,
With joy, with hope, that had no length.

This house was mine! Five hundred years
Of life and love had filled my ears,
Renewed my soul and given me eternal breath.
(The sweetest gifts from God and King were
Youth, this house, no fear of death).

I fought the French with Henry, (the Second of that name),
His gratitude was boundless, this house of glorious fame!
The years moved on in beauty, but 1642
Brought civil war and hatred, a king of weakness who
I used my strength to fight for. It ended in a coup.

A battle lost, a kingdom lost, a head and leg lost too,
And Cromwell moved in swiftly to take my house from me,
To give it to a crony, a craven, fawning flea.

But once a year a ghost stands here, (or so the people say),
Moving from the moonlight, to watch, to look, to pray.
And those who see him clearly, see the smile on his face
And hear the whispered, 'Thank you,' and then an empty place . . .

Patricia Phelan

AFTER WATCHING A DOCUMENTARY ON THE KAREN PEOPLE OF BURMA

Relentlessly they are pursued,
Their land is taken, their homes destroyed
All the things which might offer some comfort,
Are the things they must avoid.

No schooling allowed for the children
With little or no opportunity for learning
The text books like the school house
Are burning, burning, burning . . .

Acts of evil and cruelty
Which go far beyond our comprehension
So appalling, yet in the western world
They rarely get a mention.

Can we begin to imagine,
Living a life, dictated by fear?
Witnessing the rape and the torture and murder
Of those that we hold most dear?

Having nowhere - but nowhere to go
No haven - no resting place
These are just some of the unspeakable horrors
That these people have to face.

But here in the west we must face the worst horror
That mainly we are deaf to their crying
And whilst we sit complacent, in safety, with plenty
A race is dying, dying, dying . . .

Karen Link

THE TOWERS

I cannot believe twelve months has gone on
Since the incident known as nine, one, one.
The Twin Towers pointing up in the sky
Not knowing how many that day were to die
Those thankful that they weren't there
Phoned in sick or an appointment elsewhere
Now known as Ground Zero it looks like a vacant lot
But to many thousands it really is not
Memories for so many will always remain
Their lives will never ever be the same
Let's keep in our hearts those who will never reappear
People are people and fear is fear
Life has to go on that's a phrase well known
But this will never be the same in many a home.

Trevor Beach

DIRTY WAR

Crisp and light
Tragic sight
Spears and bows
Hardened foes
Dogs of war
Black and sore
Flashing lights
Wounded plights
Blood and fears
Sweat on tears
Trenches gape
Cries of rape
Children flee
Enemy see
White flag raised
Fortunes praised

Graves dug deep
Families weep
Sacred home
Children roam
Concrete laid
Houses made
A world we find
With peace in mind
Through every door
A fear of war.

R Dudley

THE OBJECTOR

Branded a coward
He refused to go to war
To take the life of another man
On some foreign distant shore

Publicly scorned cruelly mocked
Thrown in a bleak prison cell
Eardrums vibrating as the cold steel door locked
Condemned to a living hell

His the courage to stand alone
No yielding to public will
A name they will not carve in stone
For mankind he could not kill

Prison walls dark and damp
His spirit rose above
Bathed in light from a heavenly lamp
Fuelled by brotherly love

Body decaying hair silvery white
His battle nearing an end
Soul slipping silently into dark night
I proudly salute you brave friend.

Thelma Slee-Thomas

TRIBUTE TO BROTHER SIDNEY

Standing on a hill, far from good or ill,
Our memories are with you still.
A memorial made from stone,
They are not alone.
Brave souls names lie in peace,
Our love for them we can release.
The scenery takes your breath away,
They are so near, yet so far away.
Their day is done, their war is won,
But memories of them will linger on.
Dear God keep them in your care we pray
Until we meet again one day.

Joyce Hammond

THE AIR RAID SHELTER

Down to the air raid shelter we race when sirens ring
Down in the air raid shelter the children start to sing
Down in the air raid shelter still more people come
Down in the air raid shelter away from midday sun
Down in the air raid shelter we each do have our place
Down in the air raid shelter you know your neighbour's face
Down in the air raid shelter you feel the ground vibrate
Down in the air raid shelter you dread the time you wait
Down in the air raid shelter you hear the sound 'All clear'
Down in the air raid shelter the light of day you fear
Down in the air raid shelter the sound of sirens done
From out the air raid shelter we exit one by one
Destruction lay around us what once we knew as home
Is now a pile of rubble a landscape raped and torn
Brick stone and mortar the smell of burning wood
Is all that lay before us where once our homes had stood
Yet in the midst of carnage there stands a single rose
To show us out of nothing a new beginning grows.

Bilbo

ANNALIESE OF HANOVER

She was eight years very young when Tommies came to call
With combustion's greedy lung that brought the airless squall
And flak and flesh were everywhere that children fought to flee
God help us all it wasn't fair but then that is 'democracy'.

Her hair was just a sooted thatch she couldn't cough a phrase
As Teddy lay in slow dispatch on an uncontingent blaze
From Lincoln's foreign concrete the staggering terror came
To plunder from the milky teat with a bomber's moral aim.

I don't know why it was then for I was only less than one
When Kelstern sent its young men to emulsify the Hun
The Fuerwehr had no water but God the Father knew
A mother and her daughter had joined the murdered Jew

Then the Magyar watched a Boeing the Grosseman, barely hung.
Launch a mushroom glowing the Empire's rising young
Agent Orange shipped to Saigon and the unborn felt the pain
But Charlie wasn't right on so she smouldered in the rain

Quiet toddlers died in a milligram from a mustard yellow speck
Or zeroed in a baby pram for a gallon of crude respect
A twenty silvered short straw and this profanity remains
The young will die of canon law but war will hide the stains.

Francis Mcdermott

FALKLANDS' BALLAD

I'd only been married a year a day,
When the postman arrived with a letter to say.
He was wanted in the Falklands - a war he must fight
And in a few days - he was gone from my sight.

He smiled when he left me and said, 'T'wont be long'
Kissed me and told me, 'This war is all wrong'
But I am a soldier and brave I must be
For Falklands I'll fight so this land can be free.

I stood by the harbour and watched his ship sail
The tears fell like raindrops as the old siren wailed.
My heart felt so empty so sad and alone,
'God bless you my darling and bring you safe home.'

He was only a young man, no life had he seen.
And he was killed fighting on Falkland's Goose Green
Now I feel so lonely with his babe on my knee
There's many a poor wife who feels just like me.

The war we have won but my darling I lost.
Our country has gained to many families the cost.
Their young sons and husbands, never home will they come
It's lucky for many - unlucky for some.

I went to the Falklands, his grave for to see,
They gave me a medal for his bravery.
What good is a medal now my love has gone,
But I have his baby and 'Life must go on'.

M P Linney

A POEM FOR ARMISTICE DAY

Do not think of us as dead
We have only gone a little way ahead
Every year we see you mourn
And every year our hearts are torn
So do not shed another tear
We would much rather see you cheer
So now let us see you smile
Sit back and think for a while
We are not dead, we are alive like you
We did our duty, what else could we do
The enemy came, it was our turn
Our spirits they just could not burn
Our friends and loved ones we left behind
We did what we had to, to help mankind
Only our bodies died and we disappeared from view
But when you sang, we sang with you
Life is bright in this world of ours
God, you see, has mysterious powers
He does not let his children die
Like you, we did not know the reasons why
The sun went out of our lives for a while
Only to return in a different style
So now we long to share our peace with you
And tell the world our Master's words really do come true.

Sylvia Gwilt

A NATION WEEPS
(For the heroes of 11/9/2001)

A nation weeps, at the destruction of man.
Who thinks he is God! But doesn't give a damn.
He punished the innocent, for no reason at all.
With the help of others, he'll never walk tall.

You destroyed families and left children alone.
A whole world was left, chilled to the bone.
Instead of pulling a nation apart
You've made them stronger with a united heart.

Justice will grip you in the palm of its hand
And heartbroken people, will rejoice in the land.
I knew no one you took that fateful day
With my broken heart, may God's children's lives you'll repay.

I only wish it wasn't so, families torn apart.
Like a madman with a knife, you aimed right in their heart.
No religion gives a man the right, to do just what you've done
And when justice cracks it's whip you'll be the first to run.

God will place these (heroes), into his mighty hand
While the heartbroken relatives will struggle hard to understand!

Mary George

SEPT 11 2001

One year ago our lives were changed,
in just minutes not in hours,
we lost friends, families and colleagues
in the destruction of the towers.

And as hard as it has been
our lives have still gone on
but we're still waiting for the moment
of when our pain and grief is gone.

But remember all the thousands
whose lives were taken on that day
and in our hearts they'll live on
and our pain may slip away.

Stephanie Button

THE YOUNG PILOT
(For Battle Of Britain Day, September 15th)

What were your last thoughts
   As you strode out to war?
Taking leave of your loved ones,
   Whose aching hearts you bore,
The local train that sped you away,
   Your destiny to await,
As they kissed, and hugged, and clung to you,
   With no insight as to your fate,
The last vision you had of them,
   Their small figures soon to disappear,
Pinched, anxious, worry-lined faces,
   Trying so hard to hide their tears.

Leaving your home - life far behind,
   Bravely setting out for the new,
Your young thoughts cling to romantic dreams,
   Yet to England's rescue you flew,
Aged only 18, you and others, answered the call,
   And mastered your art, to a merlin's whirr,
In a few short weeks, a pilot emerged,
   Guiding a super machine, to a steady purr,
High in the blue, it soared on a stealthy course,
   The pride of the nation resting on *you*,
Hurrah! Three cheers! Your very first hit,
   Many others to follow - all in your view!

Young man, your duty done,
   May you rest in peace with the Lord,
For your aircraft never returned to base,
   And you had to lay down your sword,
But *we will remember* your sacrifice,
   In your hour of glory - may this suffice.

Julia Eva Yeardye

LETTER, FOUND ON BATTLEFIELD

The guns are silent, for a while.
What I see, breaks my heart
Friends lay still, torn apart
- Through it all, I see your smile.

I think of things I should have done
You may not have thought I cared -
All the joys, we could have shared
- As lovers, enjoying passion, and fun.

My mind was on other things, like war
I knew I would have to go
- Away from you, to fight the foe
So what more could I ask you for?

War is uncertain, I dared not speak
- Of my great love for you
Knowing what we might go through
Or if our hearts would break.

The guns are starting up anew
I pray I will survive
To hold you close, to be alive
Why didn't I tell you, I love y . . .

A R Bell

MONEY, MONEY, MONEY!

When the soil fertility dwindles away
When the crops get worse day by day
When the rivers are dead, full of pollution
When the sea's so filthy it's beyond a solution
When the trees and forests have all gone
When just a handful of animals just hang on
When there's no birds, butterflies, no bees, no honey
Only then will man realise the true value of money

Did you know that if every country in the world stopped
                                    polluting the sea today,
It would be over *100* years before it started to recover?

J A Hillas

WAR THROUGH STAGNANCY

Capitalism once again is stagnant
which happens on occasions
so now they'll make the killing fields
part of their equasion.

They are well geared for this event
with their readiness to arm
this has been their insurance
to keep their system free from harm.

They boast about their politics
though they never work out right
as all wars fought in early years
is through their economic plight

But still they use those policies
even though they always fail
it is time for the ordinary people
to take the wind from out their sails.

What maniac ever wants this life
To see a million humans slain?
It is time to have a system
That can free us from this pain.

Lachlan Taylor

SEPTEMBER IN NEW YORK

Was it real or was it fiction?
That was the world's first reaction,
Seemed like a film packed full with action,
With a cast of actors on location,
Hollywood blood and guts production
In September, in New York.

Planes exploding into buildings
Flames arising, bodies falling
Towers collapsing, everyone shouting
Young girls sobbing
Young men running
Black September, in New York.

Siren screaming, ambulance racing,
Paramedics frantically rushing,
Firemen rescuing - desperately hoping,
Praying, digging, praying, digging
Searching, searching, finding nothing,
Hopeless September in New York.

Witness being interviewed on tele
Standing still with legs like jelly
Feels a sickness in his belly
Lost for words to describe the melee
Choking, gasping, crying freely,
Shocked! September in New York.

A priest is praying for the dying
In the dust where they are lying,
Planes are grounded, no one's flying,
This is hell, there's no denying,
At home alone a mother sits sighing,
Evil September in New York.

Orphaned sons and orphaned daughters
Had working parents - they were grafters
Now sacrificial lambs - to slaughter,
Lots of tears but no more laughter
Not for some time, long time after,
Angry September in New York.

It's calmer now, the dust is settling
Everyone talking, people remembering
Their colleagues, the friends with whom they were working,
The good times, the bad and the nights spent partying,
Slowly and gradually their town is recovering,
Beautiful September in New York.

Janet Thomas

SEPTEMBER 11 2002

It was a very solemn day
No traffic about after midday!
You see it was a year ago
When all of us were remembering
Why it was a 'sadness' world-wide
Not only us two who cried
Such tragedy had happened a year ago
And why it happened no one will know
That great big country the USA
New York to be precise
Had suffered such devastation
When out of the sky
Was brought such desecration
An unknown aircraft
Had found its destination
Destroying what is called
Twin Towers, thousands
Dead now all covered in flowers
The families everywhere
Were watching today on TV
That is except, my husband and me
A strange thing happened
Here in our house, you see
At exactly 2.23
Neither of us could see TV
Would you believe
The strangest thing happened?
Believe me, it's all true
And why I am telling you
Our electricity all shut!
Yes folks *we* had
'A power cut'.

B Clark

QUANDARY

I have trouble with my conscience,
When I write my poetry,
You see I end up thinking,
That it is death for one more tree.

I cannot write of 'black and white',
(You see it's not PC!),
But it's alright to kill Iraqis'
(They're a threat to you and me!)

With millions starving in the world,
You need no longer be alone,
What difference one more mouth?
Go out and get a clone!

But don't look for help from politics,
Unless you're 'flavour of the week'
And then you're one more stepping stone,
As the glory path they seek!

Communication has shrunk the world,
Each cause just one sound-byte,
Awareness stuck on overload,
How do you pick what's right?

It is no good preaching of your fears,
The reaction's just the same,
You are tagged as one more lunatic!
Just Cassandra come again!

Topaz

REMEMBRANCE DAY

What do heroes of yesterday
Think about England and us today?
We hope they think it was worth going to war,
Seeing all that blood and gore.
They have paid their dues.
What do they think of our views?

Are they healthy views we hold?
In history books that will be told.
Our actions we hope they approve,
As all ills we try to remove.

Today a service we will conduct,
As our lives we vow to reconstruct.
Remembrance Day must bring back memories
Of pals they had to leave in cemeteries.
And thinking back to the war years
With all those tears and fears.

We *do* appreciate some gave their all
When they rallied to the call.
Those that fell before the guns,
Were all somebody's sons.

But that's all behind them now.
From war they can now take a bow.
Some will shed tears today,
Others will keep them at bay.
But all will feel deep emotion
As we try to thank them for their devotion.

Fighting for freedom was their aim.
To retain it we would fight again.
As we give three cheers
For the heroes of yesteryears
We remember it's because of them,
We have no fears.

We hope they can hear the music of the brass bands.
It's telling them that England is still in good hands.
Proud and tall she stands.
Now they have shown us the way.
From now on freedom's price *we* will pay.
I hope they are pleased with our achievement.
That was born out of their bereavement.

June Egan

FAMILY AT WAR!

I'm sitting in the corner and looking at the phone
Why can't I simply pick it up and phone Mum back at home?
The things she said still hurting I knew that some were true
But when she said them like she did, it cut me through and through.

It's not that I am stubborn, I know what's right and wrong
But sometimes we must take a stand and try to soldier on.
I wish it never happened, especially on this day
The thoughts and fears come flooding back - it never goes away.

If time could be a healer - I'd pray it could be soon
To quickly cover all this bad and heal my gaping wound.
Oh, why can't I just do it, there's something holds me back.
Why am I very frightened and fearful of attack?

So life continues daily, this year like any other
The trials and tribulations of missing my own mother
I think I may just post a card as it's now Mother's Day.
The card I chose is just plain blank, well what now can I say?

I'll send it from my doggies and put in lots of kisses
And hope the crosses on the card are ones from me she misses
If only she would call me, this happens every year
I start to write inside the card, then rub out . . . Mummy dear.

Paula Ely

A 15 YEAR OLD'S WAR

'Under the stairs'
My father said,
'That's going to be
Where we make your bed'

An old soldier he
From World War One
Had seen many times
What bombs had done.

And he wasn't wrong,
A bomb did fall
Right on our front lawn,
A very 'close call'

'Stay where you are'
Dad called, as he dressed
And hurried to see
What to do for the best.

He dashed to the Wardens
All cosy in their shed,
'Where did that one fall?'
'I'll soon show you,' he said.

They all stared in amazement,
Seeing the lawn blown up on the tiles
'Goodness what an escape you had
You could all be dead the whiles.'

And what did we do with the hole?
Well it's now a beautiful pond.
And we've forgotten that awful night,
It's gone to the back of beyond.

Joan Chapman

TORN APART

From early morn till late at night,
The lonely child is full of fright;
The shouts and screams are hard to bear,
She truly wonders if they care.

The doors are banged with mammoth force,
What is this world they call divorce?
The child's head just rocks with pain,
Oh! Please dear God, relieve the strain.

Return from school and all seems well,
My tea and chat with Mum seems swell;
When Dad comes home I feel so great,
Would they really make new date?

Alas the air soon fills with flame,
First one, then other, lays the blame;
The shouts and bangs just reach my head,
Do they really want me dead?

I close the door into my room,
The whole wide world seems full of gloom;
I jump on bed and start to sob,
Do parents know my childhood rob?

A tap on door brings call from Mum,
My sobs, so loud, have made her come;
At last she knows the stress and pain,
That Mum and Dad have caused my brain.

She shares her thoughts and listens to me,
Another tap and Dad brings tea;
We talk together, we build up trust,
The battle is over, peace is a must.

John Paulley

JULY 1997 - PRAYERS

I start my prayers with heavy heart
This world of ours is being torn apart
Dear Lord please help us all to see
This is not as it should be
You taught us how to love and care
You told us how it's good to share
Dear Lord I know you're always there
Please show us where we've gone astray
Help us back to live your way
No more wars, no more crime
Just a peaceful time, loving time
We'll learn again to love and care
But most of all we'll learn to share
And when this world of yours is free
And everyone gives thanks to thee
Then in your love we all will grow
I thank you Lord with all my heart
I know with prayers we'll get a new start.

E M Lamb

WAR/PEACE

Perhaps we must have war!
In the end to give us peace!
Peace at any price? Is that
What we've heard preached?

To maim and destroy,
To hurt, and 'toy'.
What causes such evil deed?
Power, envy, greed,
My lot, your lot,
Some have, some have not.

God why can't we be
Content with our lot!
Ah, but need wants much -
And much needs more -
At whatever cost!

War or peace!

E Montgomery

A WAR BABY REMEMBERS

I recall those austere Forties days,
As into my childhood I do gaze,
Searchlights scouring darkened skies,
A glow of wonder in my infant eyes,
Explosions and crackles like distant thunder,
Filling my mind with awe and wonder,
With fire and explosions all around,
I was carried to safety - below ground,
Air raid wardens with hats of tin,
Shouting 'Lights out!' amidst the din,
Windows covered in sheets of black,
As German bombers commenced attack,
In underground shelters we huddled in fear,
Then relief, as sirens heralded 'All clear',
Emerging in the morning from a night of trouble,
To find not our homes, but piles of rubble,
Home guards ushered us to a hall,
To gather and register for 'roll call',
They served a meal, no bacon or ham,
Just dried eggs and a piece of Spam,
No white bread for us to toast,
No chicken, pork or beef to roast,
No fresh fruit or cream for sweet,
An orange or banana a rare treat,
We queued for food, a regular habit,
How we relished the humble rabbit,
That all ended in nineteen forty five,
We came through smiling, glad to survive.

Reg Summerfield

THE WAR

Tell me what
they are fighting for?
Power and glory?
I don't think so.
I think man,
has gone crazy.
In this day and age
they must get a buzz
like the planes
buzzing in and out of the skies,
bombing everything in sight.

E Bevans

A GENTLEMAN RETIRED

See that grand old gent, standing there.
He with the quiet, distinguished air.
Note how he stands out in the crowd.
His head held high, his bearing proud.

A retired, military man no doubt!
After years of service, now passed out.
Oh, what memories must he have?
Of his long life span, from a lad.

What stories could he now unfold?
Of past actions, so brave and bold.
Of campaigns in far off foreign lands.
Over great mountains and desert sands.

To what exotic places, has he been?
And what great wonders, has he seen?
Having travelled around the globe,
He's now at last arrived back home.

I wonder if great deeds, he's done?
And has he many medals won?
It's now the time, to enjoy his rest,
After his many long years of quest.

His face, now tanned and lined with care,
Compliments his greying hair.
A man who's fulfilled his life's ambition!
Yes, a soldier of true tradition!

W A Holmes

WAR AND PEACE

Why do we have to argue?
Why do we have to fight?
Why do two wrongs
Have to make a right?

Why can't we be happy
Instead of being sad?
Why do all the things in life
Have to be so bad?

So many things are evil
Too many people sin
What's happening to this world
That we are living in?

Why can't all our enemies
Turn into our friends?
Don't you think it's time
For us all to make amends?

Sylvia Horton

FALL OUTS

Most families have fall outs,
It happens everyday,
They disagree with one another,
And cruel words they say,

This causes lots of sadness,
Those we love we hurt,
When in the heat of the moment,
Insults at each other blurt,

Anger causes heartache,
It's no good to anyone,
When it's passed you're sorry,
But the damage has been done,

Fall outs cause misery,
To those that you hold dear,
There can't be any pleasure,
Seeing loved ones shed a tear,

Take a good look in the mirror,
Are you pleased with what you see,
The face of the person,
Who partly caused this miser-ee,

So give the one that you've upset,
A great big hug and say,
'All that's gone before has passed,
Let's start anew today',

So take a long deep breath,
Your teeth if you wish may grind,
Then as you slowly let it out,
The past leave far behind.

Jack Robinson

WAR AND PEACE

I have seen both war and peace,
Hope and pray that wars can cease.
It affects all people both rich and poor,
Makes people feel very insecure.
Whether it is in Northern Ireland or Afghanistan,
It is all about power in the mind of man!
There have been wars throughout the ages,
No one understands this hate that rages.
Peace is what we can all strive for,
Whether it be far away or at our own door.
We can pray for peace and care for each other,
Be closer to God and love sister and brother.
The nations must talk and mean what they say,
We all want peace without delay.
Think of the World's children and future mankind,
This is God's world, made with God's mind.

Joyce Hallifield

SHALOM

Is peace a thing that comes from much bereavement
Do so many have to die before 'shalom'
O' peace is not a state of man's achievement
For were it so we'd have to praise the bomb
'Shalom' is what is found in Christ the Saviour
It's not some plan a government may find
And those who seek it show by their behaviour
'Shalom' is something farthest from their mind

O' would that man could see his own position
He'd know that peace and compromise won't blend
When sin remains his permanent condition
No peace can come from fences he might mend
No presidential treaty could arrange it
There's no success forthcoming from 'UN'
And negotiations made by blade or bullet
Leave all concerned in worse than Daniel's den

Shall Jerusalem belong to some pretender
O' Israel, speak out the swift reply
You only need your history, remember
Would you what God has given now deny
O' Israel, recall your known commander
Or does God no longer hear the people's cry
As soon as you restore the 'old' agenda
'Shalom' will be your portion by and by.

Alex Lawrence

MY WAR

I was a wartime evacuee, a puny little thing
With gas mask on my shoulder and suitcase tied with string.

They told me I was going to a safe and secret place.
They tied a label on my coat, another on my case

You're going to the country for a holiday they said.
Away from the bombs and air raids you'll sleep safely in your bed.

The train was at the station, the kids all in a queue.
Our mammies waved as the train pulled out
And soon were lost from view.

Some of us were crying on that bleak September day.
I thought I might jump off the train, I wondered what they'd say

There were fresh eggs in the country and apples rosy red,
But the thing I missed the most of all was our big steel shelter bed

I was a wartime evacuee, a casualty of war.
If only I'd been a little older,
Not a shy little infant of four.

Anne de Menezes

AFGHANISTAN

From a child I couldn't wait to travel about,
I saw mind blowing sights, but one country stood out.
Every part of this vast country that I saw,
Made me want to stay till I'd seen more and more.
Miles of sandy desert, rugged plains then mountain snow,
Depending on this great country to what part of it you go.
Proud, friendly shepherds, guarding their herd,
The thought of them as terrorists to me is absurd.
Russia fancied invading this land,
So in they went and took command.
After many years of occupation
The Russian left after destroying a nation
After a horrific terrorist attack
Afghanistan's troubles were soon back.
Bombs and invasion was there again,
Tribes fight back but are soon slain.
Bodies bleeding,
Injured screaming,
Horrific dreams,
Nightmare screams,
Hatred soon becomes perverted,
Even Allah has deserted.
I grieve for this country, let its people know peace,
Show some mercy, let this evil war cease.

Jan

LET, HIS LAMBS, PLAY!

Hear the children's weeping!
Wipe away their tears!
Give the comfort that they seek,
And end our 'warring' years.

Let them have only summers!
Not, harsh winters, so unkind!
Let, His lambs, in pastures, play,
Without loss of limb, or mind.

Death chants from babes' mouths!
At the ready, with gun, in hand!
A reality. To which, I will never stoop,
To accept. Or, even try, to understand.

Donna June Clift

THE ISLAND OF DREAMS

The island of dreams, where beauty abounds,
Was shaken by earthquakes, a thunderous sound.
The buildings collapsing, on top of them all,
Those poor village people, lying under the walls.

Then into the picture, after rebuilding work,
Came Venetians and French, the Britain and Turk,
To fight for the soil of this island so fair,
It never seemed right to those who lived there.

And then World War Two with all that it brought,
Italians and Germans and those that they fought,
The killing fields yonder, where bad slaughtered good,
Leaving those living in reflective mood.

To rebuild their houses and start once again,
With a shrug of the shoulders, and that heart aching pain,
Until, again came that rumbling, more panic and fear,
Another earth shaker, that cost them all dear.
But the island to this day remains in our dreams,
Cephalonia's beauty, continues, it seems.

John Cook

FORGET THEM NEVER

In November on the 11th hour of the 11th day
Let us all make a time to pray
For a wife's husband, a child's father or mother's son
Felled by the power of an enemy gun
Let us give thanks for the freedom for which our serviceman fought
And on this day we must give thought
For what they so unselfishly gave
Their lives now gone, buried in distant graves.

Gertrude Schöen

UNDERSTANDING

I wish I could say that I understand
Why innocent people must die,
So that some individuals can make a point
While the rest of the world can cry.

I wish I could say that I understand
When my faith in God is so strong.
Why murder is done for religious beliefs
And the killers can't see they've done wrong.

I wish I could say that I understand
Why people can kill for greed.
That murderers caught, go to prison for life
But within a few years, are freed.

And I wish I could say that I understand
Why so many enjoy their war.
Without a care that their country and kin
Are dying by the score.

Does anyone really understand
Why the violence is always there?
After all we're only human!
If only the guilty would care.

Christine Ash-Smith

GOD IS STILL ON THE THRONE

When wars and uprisings seem to abound,
While evil and sin are always around,
And love and peace is so hard to be found,
Remember God is still on the throne.

When from God people turn away,
No longer do they want to pray,
And very dark seems the day,
Remember, God is still on the throne.

When governments seem themselves to please,
And go on massive spending sprees,
Bringing the country to its knees,
Remember, God is still on the throne.

Although all around you looks bad,
And makes your heart feel very sad,
Here's something that will make you glad,
Yes, God is still on the throne.

P Mcalpine

UNTITLED

Those of you who kill and maim will never understand
Never ever can you hope to reach the promised land
Your targets are the innocents, the young, the old, the weak
Those of us who always have turned the other cheek.

To cause this hell and mayhem is what you most enjoy
It pleasures you to see bodies broken like a toy
You use the term 'religion' to bend others to your will
How your God must weep for the many graves you fill.

One day you will be punished for the terror and the grief
You are not a freedom fighter you are nothing but a thief
You will never reach the promised land no matter how you try
For on the day of judgement, each of you will die.

Diane L Brown

THE BLITZ

The sky is alight tonight
No birds are left in flight
An eerie silence fills the air
And yet - and yet there's something there
We were happy with our lives
Then death fell from out the skies
First to set the town alight
Then come again to destroy at dead of night

The world we knew was turned upside down
But people were brave in our dear town
With no thought of gain or glory
They dug, searched, and gave their lives
This is their story
Too old, too young, or not too well.
They spent their nights, yes nights of hell
Helping their fellow man, with just a pump
                                    or a watering can
Gallant men with hearts of gold
Now at last their story will be told.

Pat Ellwood

WAR

'Kill me if you must!' Oh mankind's greed, religious hate . . .
Oh blood-stained ethnic lust.
'Pierce this heart that beats as yours, betray God's sacred trust.'
No foreign fields are spared the blood, no home untouched by grief,
Stolen dreams and widows' tears, succumb to war, 'the thief.'
Why can't you sit and talk to me, why not deliberate?
Why must our children's laughter turn to adult hate?
Tell me these things ere I die, tell me that war is just,
Convince me war's the only way - then 'kill me if you must!'

Laurence Eardley

A TROUBLED WORLD

This troubled world we all live in
Is full of hate and full of sin.
No one will give peace a try;
Why should this be? I can't think why.

What on this Earth can we do
To help the Arab and the Jew?
Oh why do they hate each other?
In this world we are all brothers.

The suicide bomber is a threat,
Causing havoc and causing death.
If only Allah would them tell,
For this crime they'll go to Hell.

In this land, land where Jesus stood,
Who for our world did so much good,
Why don't their leaders use their might
Working for peace and not to fight?

Working together with a good will,
One another they would not kill;
With forgiveness in their hearts,
This, for them, would be a good start.

When peace comes things will be great
For the Arab and Jewish states;
When on the street they do meet
One another they will all greet.

Francis Allen

EVEN TODAY

Even in its early days . . .

This is the twenty-first century,
And along its infant days,
War has been in its ways.

The world wars still are here,
And no sign to clear
What does mankind truly care?
Some of us want lasting peace
Besides knowing how to share.

We all come in with naught,
With nothing to go out with, taught,
We see the joy of football,
It shows there is no need for war at all.

Soon there will be games
When to take their time,
On the coming joy,
Having a happy way to remember
And no world war ever.

May all around come to see the joy,
No matter what their age,
To remember the happiness
And to be shown the golden age.

Anita M Slattery

FEMALE QUARRELS

Two small girls, perfect companions
in control of their dominion.
Bodies grow rigid, smiles crumble,
quarrels on horizon rumble.

Stubborn, each believing she's right
eyeball to eyeball, faces tight.
One bristling with sheer frustration
sister oozing indignation.

Unaware he's caused the friction,
female fight with tools of diction.
Wounding words, he finds so scary
no ground's given to the unwary.

Having failed at conciliation
he gazes in resignation
watching female wrath and fury.
He won't act as judge or jury.

Can't grasp subtleties of conflict
without rule or written edict.
Harsh words an air of tension leave,
a brief taste of female intrigue!

His a world of physical fight
Conflict over, they're friends for life.
Scratches and bruises bring a smile,
badges of honour worn with pride.

He hopes that soon they'll make their peace
and the flow of angry words cease.
Victor shedding tears of sorrow
ready to make amends tomorrow.

Kathleen Potter

WHY CELEBRATE?

They told me it was done.
They told me we had won.
We had sunk the rising sun,
with a bomb, a thousand ton.

They told me no more war,
healing the sick would be the law,
houses for all, and even more.
They told me they would feed the poor.

I came back to the land that's free.
Left my friends 'neath a plantain tree.
Fifty years on, what do I see?
Hypocrisy, greed and rape for tea.

Derek Ewer

THE INTRUDER
(To Tony)

Who is causing the mischief about your place
    And leading you such a tiresome chase?
Stealing your apples, lifting the eggs from the nest,
    Teasing you for a merry jest.

Could he be a McTavish o' The Rawes?

He chases your sheep and opens your gates,
    Then leaps your hedges to join his mates.
He makes you feel so slow and dim,
    Now you'd love to get your hands on him!

Is he a McTavish o' The Rawes?

He has flaming red hair and freckles to match,
    He's hard to thole and hard to catch,
He's fleet of foot, lanky and thin.
    You'll just have to get your hands on him!

He *is* a McTavish o' The Rawes!

Now he's made friends with the young folk.
    The boys are talking about you and his granda - a huge joke!
The girls say he's a bit of a hoot!
    Though, young Emma thinks he's real cute!

Their granny says that the lad is OK.
    She took him in and gave him his Tay.

A McTavish o' The Rawes in your house taking his Tay!

She says it's time to settle the old score,
    That the feud between you and oul' McTavish is now just a bore.

'Two oul' men, thinking they're brave,
    Fighting over a woman, long in her grave!
And she married neither of them - wise Kate!
    But left us, who did, with this legacy of hate!'

Now you see - they're all ganging up on you,
And - banded together - thy're a tough crew!
So you'll need a horsewhip, or even a gun,
To put young Alistair McTavish on the run!

Mary Agnes Elliott

A PEACE WITHIN

Let not your mind be as a babbling brook
But let it be a place of calm and still
Turn slow, to read each page within life's book
To find and know, the purpose of God's will.

So many things must be as they must be
They will not change, no matter how you try
For you will only find serenity
If you accept and seek no reason why.

Yet there are many things that you can do
To nourish that which is your spiritual wealth
Each thought and action which is part of you
Can be for others and in turn yourself.

Then you will know the spirit that's within
That peace of mind which fills your heart and soul
A pact with God, you make, when you begin
To realise, that each is part of whole
That every human on this Earthly plane
That knows itself by colour, creed or race
Is but a spark of God's Eternal Flame
A light of love which shines in darkest place.

So open up the portals of your mind
And let this glorious light of love shine through.
Keep faith within your heart and will find
That peace within; the love of God for you.

'Father anoint the troubled waters of men's minds
With you oil of love.' To bring a peace within and
Thus create peace throughout this Earthly place.

T McAllister

40 YEARS AGO

Tell me what was in your heart
Those 40 years ago
That damp November night
The gas turned on and left to flow.

And how slick to leave no note,
A question in the air
Unanswered still today,
What filled your soul with such despair?

Tell me what was on your mind
When all seemed well before,
We thought that you'd got well
From complications with the war.

Would that I had seen the signs
And spent more time with you,
Would that have stayed your hand
Or harden more your saddened view?

You have nothing to regret,
You fought a hungry foe
And in the end you won,
Something, those 40 years ago.

L K Clements

SHADOWS

*(Written in 2000 after the end of another inflammatory,
hate-filled marching season)*

Should Romans yearly strut our streets,
to mark their triumphs past,
reminding of long-gone defeats,
what shadows would be cast?

Should Polish lanes and fields of France
feel once again the blast,
and tremble to the jack-boot's dance,
what shadows would be cast?

Should allies, marching every year
reliving glories vast,
reopen wounds and pain and fear,
what shadows would be cast?

Destroy your drums, you marching men,
bring flags down from the mast.
The future's bright. Just start again.
Leave shadows in the past . . .

Pack up your pipes, you marching boys,
your time is fading fast.
Turn to the sun. Just stop your noise.
Leave shadows in the past.

Your children can be saved. Here's how . . .
make last year's march your last.
It's up to you. Just do it . . . now!
Leave shadows in the past.

Phil Austin

NORTHERN IRELAND

Belfast can be a strange place
with a southern or Scottish face.
No-go areas of a town street
where communities never meet,
unless to throw lethal bombs
amongst innocent throngs.
My father always said:
and he had a good sane head,
'Britain should let them fight it out
amongst themselves whatever the bout!'

Ursula Meldon

WAR AND HOPE

War cannot steal each moment's loveliness.
Loneliness and parting cannot interpose
Between the soldier and his joy, their barrenness,
Or tear from the grower his imagined rose.
Even the sacrificed slain
Must from their mountains aspire
Out of death and out of pain
To the pure immortal fire.
Oh suddenly the soldier's day
Turns to an ecstasy, follows a way
From war to God's eternal light
That changes now his human sight.

Uvedale Tristram

BOMBING BETHLEHEM

What are names for, if never to be used
Sharon of Israel only known to a few
Suddenly millions know his act of terror
Bombing Bethlehem his most dastardly error
Shelling and killing defenders within
UN declared withdraw your dastardly sin
Sharon replied murdering more and more
United Nations exposed to the core.

Bombing Bethlehem an unimaginable thought
Religious leaders totally shocked and fraught
United they stand within Bethlehem to defend
Against Gun-Ho from the west killing with zest
While people, humanity and life seemingly depend
On politicians with little beginning and no end
In time of war not in the front always the rear
High and mighty return to Blighty seeking cheer
'We've heard it all before,' some would say

But if it's World War Three, the end is nigh
Because God's own Palestine will never die.

W C Pafford

THEY BRANDED ME A COWARD

I'd been a young man, filled with life, at a very innocent age,
I was caught up in my national pride; I'd fight the German rage,
So a soldier boy I then became, to wear the kilt with pride,
They sent me to a foreign land, where my body would soon reside.

With a shovel, a gun and bayonet, to the hellish front was sent,
Where blood and lice were normal, my life to our king I'd lent,
Would the end be in a muddy hole, would I see my eighteenth year,
In the screaming hell, the tortured souls lay in the mud in fear.

They lay so still with staring eyes, chests labouring hard for air,
No one could sleep in this hellish place, where men lay in despair,
The men were like the living dead, no feelings in their bodies left,
Where the zombies lay with sightless eyes, their sanity now bereft.

Deep in my heart, my fear was stark; there was thunder in my head,
I cringed deep down within my tomb, my body so filled with dread,
The deadly shells came screaming, at tortured souls cowered down,
And killed the shell-shocked soldiers, that lay huddled on the ground.

An officer stood and screamed at me, my ears could hear no sound,
He pointed his loaded revolver at my head, to hellfire I was bound,
They took me to a court martial, where they branded me a coward,
They sent me to a coward's grave, where Flander poppies flowered.

I'm dwelling up in Heaven now and I watch the peaceful land,
I was put here in this holy place, by my nation's vicious hand,
The verdict they said was cowardliness, they said my nerve had gone,
So they tied me to a shooting pole and they shot me dead at dawn.

Sandy Laird

WAR

Wars and rumours of war from beginning of time
Has degraded this world - so much proof we find
In our history books - power, hatred and selfishness
Has always been a threat to mankind.

During the First World War in France they dug trenches
And a chaplain was there - 'Woodbine Willie' by name
He saw warfare first-hand - in all its grim aspects
Later becoming a poet of fame.

He wrote a poem wherein he acclaimed that war
Was a waste of muscle, manhood, beauty and health
Also of patience, tears and youth's most precious years
God's glory and man's blood, brain and wealth.

The heartbreaking results which war leaves in its tracks
Is not easy to estimate - how can one know
The ultimate consequences that can accrue
Which may not immediately show.

If only mankind - the wide world over - could learn
To live in harmony, contentment, love and peace
Then all the dissension and devious dealings
Which make wars on the earth - would cease.

Greta E Bray

NEW JERUSALEM

'An eye for an eye and a tooth for a tooth.'
Where will it end?
Israel drives tanks into the Gaza Strip:
Arab mothers send
Their sons as martyrs, on suicide missions.
No attempt to mend
Relationships, to respect each other's faith.
It seems they intend
To bomb, kill and maim, until their enemies
No longer defend
Their countries, families, friends, beliefs and hopes.
Where will it end?

Jesus walked among those arid hills and preached
A Kingdom of Peace:
Political peace between Roman and Jew
When hatred would cease;
More significant: love between God and man.
Jesus wept for peace,
In Jerusalem, in the hearts of all men,
In a world where police
And fighting men have no place. Love will take over.
With the decease
Of sin and fear, all men will love their neighbour.
Then there will be peace.

Since history began, we have searched for peace:
Men have fought for it,
Women have longed for it.
Jesus said, 'Love your enemies, pray for them'.

Where could that end?

Shirley Boyce

THE INNOCENTS

The sun shone brightly on the day
The world would witness its betray
The hate that filled the morning sky
Left innocents alone to die
Brave hearts wept at Ground Zero
The city's mayor a world hero
To all of those who passed away
On that tragic September day
We pray the world will overcome
Its loss and grief for everyone
But God takes care of those who die
And angels watch where heroes lie
And one day we will see the light
Of peace on Earth for all that's right
I pray one day that we may see
A world at peace where all are free
We stand in silence to recall
The innocents who gave their all.

Frank Osborne

THE WHOLE WORLD STOPPED
(Dedicated to K.T. survivor of the New York terror)

A bright sunny morn, in the city called New York,
As the people start early, they drive as they talk,
Preparing themselves for the hours ahead,
While the rest of the world is tucked up in bed,

The madness and panic of everyday lives,
As workers leave their houses, kissing their wives,
Wishing their children goodbye as they go,
And head into work, for a day that is slow,

They drive to the office, a towering block,
A sight to amaze, and to some it does shock,
The twin towers so high, gleaming so bright,
Under the yellow and orange sunlight,

Taking the elevator with briefcase in hand,
To their various jobs their bosses demand,
The building fills up with so many faces,
People of all age, all sexes and races,

They all set about their daily tasks,
Just a hard day's work is all that is asked,
So many people with jobs of all types,
Working so hard to get by in their lives,

With the hustle and bustle of another work day,
A moment of madness takes all lives away,
A person so cruel, who's all full of hate,
Leaving people no warning, for them it's too late,

An exploding sound brings the work to a halt
As a plane hits the tower, like a lightning bolt,
The whole building shakes from the top to the ground,
People are screaming, 'There's fires around,'

So many people lost, or injured so bad,
By some evil person, who is clearly mad,
Who suffers a sickness inside his head,
To hurt so many people and so many dead,

The panic and hurting as the silence kicks in,
The whole world stops with a deafening din,
Four planes fall down, right out of the sky,
And crash into those buildings standing so high,

The buildings crash down, just like my heart,
As I watch things in motion from miles apart,
So many are trapped, under buildings they stay,
As slowly their lives are drained all away,

I feel so deeply for the people who are lost,
Nothing on earth is worth such a cost,
The memories of those who have lost their lives,
Will always live on in their children and wives,

In their family and friends this tragedy remains,
I will remember this for the rest of my days,
Everyone is shocked by this tragic event,
In our hearts and our minds it places a dent,

We will never forget this most tragic day,
As the moment we saw it, our breaths went away,
We all pull together, we all act so brave,
With so many people lost, we've yet to save,

My thought go out to all those who died,
And the rescue services who have struggled and tried,
To save many people, they've worked night and day,
In our hearts, their courage will stay . . .

Mitch Cokien

THE DREAM

I had a dream of paradise,
where life was peaceful, serene.
There was no chaos or pollution,
everywhere was green and clean.
My sons weren't dressed in uniforms,
helping to keep the peace.
No country was fighting each other,
wars had come to cease.
Animals weren't chased and hunted,
no birds were shot for pleasure.
Mankind wasn't greedy and grasping,
money and material goods their treasure.
Every morning was a joy to wake to,
each day was a joy to live.
It was a pleasure to be with
people who had so much love to give.
If only my dream of this paradise
would become a reality,
not disappear when I open my eyes
and I'm back to being the same old me.

Patricia Gray

SLAUGHTER OF THE INNOCENT

There was a silence in the churchyard
when the service was done.
Helpless tears of anguish
ran down the cheeks of everyone.

Robbed of their loved ones,
numbed by their pain,
the few remaining town folk
stood huddled in the rain.

No one can ever justify
the wrong that has been done.
Those soldiers running carefree
bringing death to every home.
Leaving a landscape of carnage
in a war which nobody has won.

Why us? What did we do to you?
We ploughed the land and tilled the corn,
working tirelessly day and night,
never ceasing from our toil
until we bore fruit
from our now blood-soaked soil.

Old and young, maimed and poor,
slaughtered like cattle on their own front doors.
And what was your reason?
It was all in the name of war.

E McGrath

WAR AND TRUTH

I was just a boy when the war began
But I wanted to be a soldier
I wanted to be a man

My grandpapa he tried to stop me
Do you know what you are fighting for?
'For Truth,' I said. And Glory was all I saw

He took me by the shoulders
And stared into my eyes
Child, Truth can be lies in disguise

'The Truth, my boy, can be a subjective thing
One man's gaoler; another man's king
A bittersweet nectar for which so many thirst
The burden under which so many curse.'

Yet I ignored him and took up my arms
A child with a gun
A game of soldiers, shooting would be fun

I saw man's blood
I felt man's pain
And I smelt man's death again and again

I fought for the promise of the Truth
I starved for the promise of the Truth
I traded my childhood for the promise of the Truth

And as death approaches, I have found a very different Truth.

Catherine Fleming

WAR IN PEACETIME (SEPTEMBER 11TH)

What is this hatred?
As a cancer consumes the body, it eats away at the mind and soul.
We ask, 'How can they do this?'
Who knows? We cannot tell.
We know that they caused a living hell.
What is it that flashes from their eyes? Is it sadness?
No. Surely it's madness.

The loathing that lies within their mind burns as a hot poker,
Scarring the heart. They smile as the misery they inflict.
Tolls the death knell for many.
No quarter given to any.
This, we must all rise above . . .
We must remember love.

'In the name of God,' they cry. I think not.
Can they not see? 'Tis in no one's name but that of Satan.
The Devil himself.
No permit, no sanction
From any god for this action.
Evil is this, evil does. Innocents, snuffed as candles in the wind.

No hope for them now, just the hereafter.
The grief left behind them. So deep goes the sorrow.
This also can eat at the soul.
We must not let these feelings burn as a coal
To breed the same hatred as theirs.
Or we too are lost.
Too great is that cost.

Ann J Thorpe

TEARS OF STEEL
(Italy, Montecassino Memorial)

To the baying dogs of war,
To those who want to rule the world
Through avarice and greed,
Priceless is its message to conflicts
Unholy deeds.

These tears of steel
Proclaim from the hillside,
Proclaim to the skies,
Proclaim for the memory
To those who endeavoured and died.

Some would say what was done
Was a terrible waste,
And what was achieved filled
Others with distaste.
The man who gave the order
To bomb, he was one of Hollywood's
Movie actor greats.

But while history has taught us
There are no winners, only losers in war,
In many parts of the world today
The hounds of Hell are baying once more . . .

Peter Morriss

WAR - WHY?

Think about the children whose lives don't bring a smile,
Do we ever stop and think, just for a while?
Many tears are spilt with missiles flying by,
Children of the war, they're so unaware why.
The senseless slaughter, sons and daughters,
Innocent victims caught in a tangle of torture.
Devastation everywhere, the family circle broken, scattered and
                                                    in despair,
The inner strength to keep on going is slowly slipping away.
God give us strength for another day, they pray.
The victim's circle keeps on going, feelings of hate keep on growing,
On and on, the war goes strong.
Why? When this is all so wrong!

Karin Edwards

LIVING IN HOPE

When man destroys his fellow man
what hopes are there for peace,
how can they be such hypocrites
when they say that war will cease,
can we not live in a peaceful world,
or is that too much to ask,
when leaders of the powers-that-be
make it so great a task?

When one supplies the other
with firearms untold,
financial gain is their only aim,
when greed has taken hold,
if we could just replace the hate
that fills so many a mind,
with love and understanding
soon a peaceful world we'd find.

Then, when all the wars have ended
and the greed has gone away,
we could then all share together
a brighter, hopeful day.
But, when we hear of 'arms control'
can we be really sure
that there isn't someone out there
who can't wait to wage a war?

J W W Griffiths

WHY WAR? WHAT FOR?

The boy said to the man
'Were you in the war? And what was it for?
What is a war?'
'It's for medals son, that's what I won!'
'Does everyone get medals then?' said the boy
'And what about bombs, don't they destroy?'
'Oh yes, they do, and lots of lives too.
They get destroyed, that you can't avoid.'
'Well, what about food and houses and clothes,
Do people get more, or do they stay poor?'
'Oh yes, they stay poor, they're robbed to the core
Of all their possessions and a lot more,
Families are broken, often wiped out,
Babies are orphaned, reason in doubt
Of why we need these cruel, bloody wars.
When families are torn, the losses they mourn
And cities are shattered, destroyed and battered.'
'Well then,' said the boy, 'why is there war,
Why should it be?'
'Well son, it's a desire to be free,
But when all said and done, it's just medals, you see.'

Gillian Browning

D-Day

Worse than a nightmare – the Second World War
nobody grasped what was in store
no nation apprehended what has occurred
- their visions were blurred -
nobody grasped that a monster arose
annihilation of humanity was close.

That nightmare had lasted for many years
it fed on more than millions of tears
that irrigated stretches of earth
where victims were buried even prior to birth.

The war ended at long last
D-Day came - fifty years have passed
atrocities, though, have left their mark
their cruelty unbelievably hard to impart.

Whoever emerged alive from that hell
should never cease assiduously to tell
and warn all future generations
to keep mutual watch over all nations . . .

Wila Yagel

REMEMBER THEM

We will remember them,
On this day so chill,
They stand close beside us,
And they always will.

We gather here to praise them,
Their valiant deeds we know.
Some rest in places far away,
But their legends tend to grow.

We wear a scarlet poppy
To show how much we care.
The poppies blaze with honour,
Our thoughts are with them there.

They cannot hear the bugle,
Or see the pennants fly.
But they are part of us today,
And tears will fill the eye.

So wear your poppy full of pride,
Although it brings regret.
And with the heroes you will stand,
On this day you won't forget.

Duchess Newman

A MOTHER'S SON

When I grow up
I'll be a soldier
My son he said
To me
When I grow up
I'll be a soldier
As brave and proud
As I can be.
When he grew up
He was a soldier
As brave and proud
As he could be
But on a street
In Northern Ireland
They took his life
Away from me.

Christopher S Mills

THE GREAT WAR 1939 – 1946

I am now an airman in Air Force blue
Given a number, which is quite new
I shout it out to get my pay
Then remember, it was a shilling a day
I tendered the planes whilst on the ground
So that they took to the skies around
Fighters, bombers, come what may
It was my job, almost every day
Except when I was given leave, time for a rest
I can assure you, I did my best
I watch with envy, the planes up high
All eyes looking upwards to the sky
Where are they going? We were never told
Will they ever return to the fold?
Those that did had tales to tell
Of how their comrades went through hell
It was no picnic, was always the cry
As one by one they left the sky
Reinforcements are on their way
Piloted by maidens so they say
Not one, not two, but quite a band
Our fleet at last can now expand.

Walter John Coleman

BEST SILENCE SPEAK
(Belsen Camp, 18th April 1945, two days after occupation by British Second Army)

Best silence speak - misdeeds have always been
Retold in words already out of date,
And could we make for those who have not seen
This thousand, thousand dead articulate

Their mandibles, agape or shut, hold fast
As merciful an anonymity
As though impenetrable shroud had passed
Across the face of their humanity.

Enough that yesterday they cried too late
For any succour from this earth-bound ring
Of bent meridians impotent to rate
The measure of the worth of suffering.

Enough that blood once coursing through their veins
Lies frozen now in disconnected strands;
Only the riddle of their lives remains
Trapped in the clench of their contorted hands.

So let us leave them - free in prison rags;
Their farewell kiss the quicklime and the cold;
From foes released, by friends unmarked or flags;
Their last soliloquy in silence told.

Edward Smyth

SONS OF YESTERDAY

Where are the sons of yesterday?
Those that lived and died
And with honour did obey
Their call to arms so brave
Having just left childhood
No time had they to live
Fighting for the greater good
With only lives to give
Before their ears had dried
And for mothers they had cried
All to no avail
For the final nail
To close the coffin lid on
And all the horror hidden
Far from mothers' eyes
Eyes that could only cry
The tears of mothers' love
The tears that never dry
For their hearts forever broken
For their sons forever taken
A mother's love will never die
But remain within their souls
To the end of all eternity.

K K Campbell

THE BLITZ ON LOWTH ROAD, SE5

The sky was red, smoke filled the air
Bombs were dropping on London town.
I stood, a child of nine, half in-half out of the gap that was the door
Of an iron hut, half in-half out of the earth.
Marrows growing atop, children growing within.
Wide-eyed at the flames in the sky I said
'Dad, what's popping and that terrible smell?'
He said, 'Vinegar bottles exploding in the heat
In the factory White Cottels.'
It stood at the end of our long street
Glass exploding, smell escaping and amongst the hell
It had the air (for a moment) of a fairground
Pop guns, confusion, excitement, why I could not tell.
To me the terror became stark reality that day
My childhood pal, Roy Francis, with his brother dead he lay.
The day before we played a game on the steps of our tall house
I was the nurse, he the hero, wounded soldier, groused
He did not want the bandages, or the grubby sling
But the game was played, imagination - everything.
Now this was real, he was no more, a child of tender years
That day I cried, felt guilty and wept most bitter tears.
His family owned a barber's shop, a small and compact place
It was no more, just rubble, gone without a trace.
Now the tragedy unfolds, a bomb his shelter found
Both boys inside, his mum was told as she lay on the ground
'Your boys are both together, in hospital they lie'
Evasion of the awful truth, the little, sad, white lie.
I will never forget the day I grew up with heavy heart,
The dust, despair, a childhood memory stings and sharply smarts.
A guilt that's always been there, his face I'll always see
A game came true so tragically and took my friend from me.

Sylvia Reynolds

FREE AT LAST!

Open the door and release
Chain up the dogs and tell all police
That I am free and so shall be
The right to form the ANC

Send out the signals and tell the crowd
I still have hope and shout aloud
That there is still hope for all
For equality at large, not small

Tell your leader, we can lead
Our own lives, we too can read
That it's time to throw away the key
And tell the world Mandela's free!

Sally Watson

OUR WORLD

Why must this world be so full of friction
Squabbles and arguments and confrontation?
Drugs, racism, envy and greed
We're all human beings come colour or creed.

We're conceived and born exactly the same
Be we humble servant or royal queen.
Beggar, road sweeper, lord or king
Procreation to all is a natural thing.

Things belong to others, they're not ours
So we must have them, hence the wars.
Shooting, maiming, killing and extinction
Just because we covet someone else's possession.
What's happened to friendship, loyalty and trust
A caring hand to help where it must?

It's a beautiful world for all to enjoy
Not blow to pieces just to destroy
Because it belongs to somebody else.
Let's build a pathway to common sense
Across sea and mountains, deserts and valleys.
Let's work to protect it and all become allies.

Edith Ellen Angove

DAY BY DAY

Whatever has happened to this world we're living in?
Greed, war and drugs have become its ruin
Day by day we're faced with this harsh reality
Highlighted by our newspapers, then of course TV

Why is it greed consumes us all individually
Like a disease coursing through our veins
Changing everyone's personality
Except for those who will never know
The ones in abject poverty, the minority
No new day brings any relief for them
From their misery

Wars are wholly destructive
What makes man aggressive?
Why is there so much hate and oppression?
What makes fighting a solution?
It's always the innocent who are its victims
And the perpetrators that make themselves the martyrs

Drugs have become a scourge on our society
What makes us humans fall prey
To temptations such as these?
Why can't our innermost mind project
The havoc that they wreak?
And the mirror of our soul reflect
The pain and sadness it will bring to one's families

No answer to life's ignominities . . . do I see
Why must this world in turmoil be?
Does someone out there hold a key
Testing us all for endurability
Will it ever one day cease
And peace return with happiness?

Valerie Thompson

SEPTEMBER 11TH

One can remember the tragedy of yesterday
So surreal, but it won't go away.
It seemed so fictional
But was more so contradictional
Violence doesn't make peace.
So many innocent people lost their lives
And the world was left asking so many 'whys?'

Bethan Groves

UNFINISHED

And still the columns march along
With banners at the head;
Ten thousand of the living,
Ten million of the dead.

They died to rid the world of war
They died to make us free
Yet we prepare ten billion deaths -
Not counting you and me.

Jim Badman

New Lives For Old

How we long to start again
Not to make the same mistakes
but we find it is impossible
We haven't got what it takes

We have lived our lives so selfishly
It was always, 'what about me?'
And now the guilt is too much to bear
We want out, we want to be free.

There's only once place where we can go
Where freedom and peace is found
It's only Jesus the Saviour
Who can turn our lives around.

Christine Williams

EVACUATED

I was nine years old when it started,
And taken away from my home.
Dumped in the middle of nowhere
With plenty of space to roam.

A new school I had to get used to,
Walking three miles a day to and fro.
Trudging through snow right up to my knees,
No buses to ride, what a blow.

My long stay with my gran'ma
Only glimpsing my parents now and then.
I spent three years in the countryside,
Until the time I could go home again.

Back to my old school I returned,
Glad to be back in a town,
To civilisation with its bustle and noise
Was better than wearing a frown.

I welcomed each birthday as it came along
From nine to fifteen I did slowly pass,
From a little girl to a grown-up young lady
And considered to be not a bad looking lass.

Dangers were many, times sometimes hard,
But muddling through, our intention.
We all stuck together in all sorts of weather
Without trying to give it a mention.

The sounds of sirens and gunfire
Were all too real to ignore.
Six years of my life had been taken
To have lived through the Second World War.

Jean Naseby